Many Ways to Say It

Many Ways to Say It

poems by

Eva Saulitis

 RED HEN PRESS | *Pasadena, CA*

Book design and layout by Ina Jungmann

Library of Congress Cataloging-in-Publication Data
Saulitis, Eva, 1963–
  Many ways to say it : poems / by Eva Saulitis.—1st ed.
    p. cm.
  ISBN 978-1-59709-242-5 (alk. paper)
  I. Title.
  PS3619.A82325M36 2012
  811'.6—dc23
                    2012003711

The Los Angeles County Arts Commission, the National Endowment for the Arts, the Los Angeles Department of Cultural Affairs, the James Irvine Foundation, and the Ahmanson Foundation partially support Red Hen Press.

   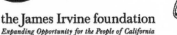

First Edition
Published by Red Hen Press
www.redhen.org

ACKNOWLEDGEMENTS

The following poems appeared, sometimes in different versions, in the places listed below. Heartfelt thanks to the editors for their support and faith:

The Alaska Quarterly Review, "It Begins in Ice," "Song of the Jealous Bird"; *Carnet de Route,* "Many Ways to Say It"; *Cimarron Review,* "The Nameless Bird," with the title "If I Speak (For the Earth)"; *Crazyhorse,* "If Only the Mind," "You Darkness"; *Ice-Floe,* "Instructions to the Husband," "What Endures," "Study."

Several poems were inspired by the works and ideas of other artists:

"Naturalist's Prayer" is after Ilya Kaminsky's "Author's Prayer," from *Dancing in Odessa.* "You Darkness" is after Rainer Maria Rilke's poem of the same name. "Burn Line" was written in the painting studio of Asia Freeman. The italicized lines are from the journals of Colette. "Sings the Self in All Her Chains" was inspired by conversations with the painter Karla Freeman. "The Clearing" owes its existence to Barbara Ras.

"Cordelia, Disobedient, Sings Her Songs": My debt to Shakespeare's *King Lear* and particularly the sonnets is large. Ever at my side was my father's 1901 Booklovers Edition of Poems and Sonnets by William Shakespeare, published by the University Society of New York. Beside that was Eric Hulten's *Flora of Alaska and Neighboring Territories* (Stanford University Press, 1968) from which the botanical language was lifted. The particular fragments from Shakespeare's sonnets incorporated into individual poems are as follows:

III: "beguile the world," "when the lusty leaves disappear," "count black fair"

XIII: "ever fixed sign," "subtle whore," "hot, hot, and moist," "come lay with me and be my," "which rack of goodness would by ill"

XI: syntax closely follows Shakespeare's CXII

IX: The opening was inspired by the title of Cyrus Cassell's collection *Soul Make a Path Through Shouting,* Copper Canyon Press, Port Townsend, Washington, 1994.

"And God Opened a Window": The last line of this poem and the title of the poem, "This is the Far-Off Country I'm Writing to You From," are derived from "I am writing to you from a far-off country," by Henri Michaux, translated by Richard Ellmann, from *Selected Writings.*

"Ghazal Of A Madman's Child" owes its existence to Zack Rogow.

"My Mountain" was inspired by the film *My Mountain Song 27* (1968) by Stan Brakhage.

"Mother Water" was inspired by a textile sculpture by Jane Regan.

More gratitude:

For reading and listening and responding to earlier drafts of poems: Arlitia Jones, Maureen Clark, Lisa Linsalata, Peggy Shumaker, Jo Going, Margaret Baker, Liz Bradfield, Derick Burleson.

For creative inspiration: The Freeman women, Shirley Timmreck, Michael Walsh, Miriam Elizondo, Margaret Baker, Kristine Rawert, Mr. P., Sherwin Bitsui, Liz Bradfield, Margo Klass, Frank Soos, Ieva Balode, Jo Going, Peggy Shumaker, Arthur Sze, James Stevens, Allison Hedge-Coke, Todd Boss, Linda McCarriston, Anne Caston, Jerah Chadwick.

For incalculable literary support: Kate Gale, Mark Cull, and Red Hen Press.

For a place to write: The women of Ventspils House, Latvia.

For financial support: The Alaska State Council on the Arts, the Rasmuson Foundation.

For sense and sensibility: My mountain, my place, my family.

For my life: Craig Matkin, Lowell Schnipper, Asja Saulitis, Jon and Mara Liebling.

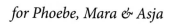

for Phoebe, Mara & Asja

CONTENTS

Many Ways to Say It

I wonder about this concept of self-control and whether it really is, as the Greeks believed, an answer to most questions of human goodness and dilemmas of civility. I wonder if there might not be another idea of human order than repression, another notion of human virtue than self-control, another kind of human self than one based on dissociation of inside and outside. Or indeed, another human essence than self.

—Anne Carson, from "The Gender of Sound"

1. AS WITNESS, AS PRAYER,
AS ANIMAL CRY

*A landscape appears before us, solitary in its incidents of meadow
broken by low running water, the sky dour, the earth in twists moving
like water into continuous dark drainage. This landscape appears
solitary and yet there in the short grass is the hidden person placed there
by the writer who desired a human instrument to bear witness . . .*

—Barbara Guest, *Forces of Imagination*

NATURALIST'S PRAYER

after Ilya Kaminsky

If I speak for the earth I must sing.

I must sing the same song every morning, sing

like the unidentified bird with its repetitive

cry, that nameless bird in the morning

who bleats & bleats like a lamb of

the wild. If I speak I must crawl

along its convergences:

> slough &
> forest & forest & floodplain & floodplain &
> > meadow & meadow & delta   collecting data:

Transcribing the falling,

the hardening. The wet, the cautious.

the curious quick licks of an animal

at the furthest

edge of its range, pressing its pads

deep into groundcover, marking

trees with its foreign scent,

its foreign name. If sing it's because

the earth persists & this is just my brief

wandering between

trees alive & dead & fallen, on all

fours through the under-story. To breathe

in a windstorm is singing. To sing is to praise

Earth's madness, placing

carefully as a predator my tread

upon each, the darkest,

the coldest. It's like dying each time,

not crazy to pray: Let this day, earth,

let it be given.

Injured and blistered amen.

INTERROGATION

Sparkler ——— heracleum stalk ——— plucked
        from the field
            in March ———this
                                   Explosion ———
umbrella-shaped   (without the skin)

umbel gale-stripped ———of flower, petal, leaf, stem, sepal ———
        stalk
            parched
                    (the way the green was long ———)
                    (the way the green was given ———)

to brown
     ———to underbark chewed pencil-thin ———worry stick ———
         (sick with waiting)
                    the heartwood ———
                      the dry-rot, the ———

Seeds cling, elliptical, flat to the armature ———

What were you doing in the vacant lot
     behind the waterfront pub that night last March?
                       Tell me that

MAYBE I'LL (GO)

Maybe at dawn I'll scan the slopes for him
from the bedroom window, hear only
his receding yips and one long
narcissistic yowl. Maybe the day coming on
will erase him, swipe the dark between trees
with its dusty rectangle.

And maybe tonight he'll come back. In bed,
I'll be reading, flash-lit
under the sheet
while my loved one sleeps.
He'll arrive at the appointed spot,
at the agreed-upon hour, wait his minute
and lope away. Maybe my heart will seize
for wanting to go with him like water
seizing into ice.

Maybe in the morning I'll do the math
of his yaps, of missed pleasure blossoming
at the edge of everything
familiar. Maybe I'll sing. *Last night I had
the strangest dream.* Of the woods
I thought I knew so well. I'll shed
my flannel and sleep-breath,
maybe I'll drink coffee.

Or maybe I'll stand on the edge of the gulch,
stare into the trees, the handle of the empty

compost pail cold on my palm.
Maybe he'll be curled in some stinking den,

some urine-pocked pit
in the snow, quick rhythms
lifting his ribs, nose stuffed into belly fur.
Dreaming what?
Maybe God knows.

There's a woods in my brain,
I think I know. I don't know.
There's someone who goes,
and she's not me. She leaves
the bucket under the tree,
follows the tracks he's trampled for her
in the decomposing snow.

SWAMP CHILD

It leads to the swamp, the trail she mapped
plant by plant, plaque by plaque, walked
the families down with her
naturalist talk. Today alone she sits on the ground
and yes, she has her logbook, her lens,
her rapidograph pen, but she doesn't
observe anything now, offers no interpretation.
Dear You, she writes:

Dear You, I read your note
 this morning, announcing
yourself, your bizarre script
on that test strip, ghosted up
when I dipped it into a cup of my pee,
my sister reading over my shoulder.
Dear You, whom I am about to kill,
we're here at the swamp,
 the two of us, reading the signs
 I wrote and pasted to planks: see
the maidenhair fern, the pond lily,
 duck weed, bird track
in the mud bank. The humidity,

a gel in which sounds gather: gasps, rapping
of a pileated woodpecker, rasp of
heron, plunk
of something water-born flung up,

then swallowed back in, the thing
she just missed seeing.
Hear the undertone, the slow reverb:
blisters on swamp-skin,

green world sprouting
islets of frog eyes, *hushaby,* she sings,
swing slow-mo like the step
of the heron's foot, a drip
off the leg that crooks
and rises, let's sleep and forget awhile.

(The swamp is listening).

Dear You: (here's where she cries,
pities herself, here's where she asks
for absolution:).

Dear Pollywog, Dear Insect,
 metamorphosing larva raining
your encasings and forms, already
changing . . .

If only I could drop you
like a premature fawn, your death-bed
a patch of liverwort and lichen, death-song
a waistband of rustling, the swamp's
surround-sound. I could say you died here,
and all the rest's just a script

I have follow, like a car crash victim
who's seen God but has to go back
among the living pretending
to be skeptical

        (the legs spread,
        the feet in stirrups, the shot
        of oblivion in her arm, nurse
        taking her hand, saying no
        it didn't hurt, it was as big
        as a fingernail paring).

Dear You, Swamp Child, stay,
live here, making your small,
aquatic sounds. Be that ear
in the ground. Be a shiver
along the skin
of some naturalist's arm.

BEFORE THE GRACE OF YOU GO I

When I lay flat on you
like a specimen in a press
cheek deep in the damp mushroom
smell of you, when I splay my toes
in your muskeg, dig my fingers in
your pelt, flowers faded, mostly, away, skeletal
lichens spidering this
small hummock topped by gale-flattened
spruce there's nothing
I need. Willingly, I would shed all but
these old clothes. Twist me
inside out like prey. Examine, dissect
catalogue me. And I will eat
your saltbush, your quillback fish,
your sulfur fungus arrayed on the dead
tree. I will gnaw the bones
of your drowned deer. When I go,
may I be pregnant from our animal
love on the streambed and on the bluff.

BURN LINE

for Asia

If wildfires singe the moon orange,
revise the way we see water,

then linseed, varnish, turpentine
make the oil act like water,

revise the way we see fire. At least
that's what she's after: the landscape

to say: the gluey clouds inking
down, that Prussian line along the taiga.

Just as the Inupiaq won't predict
weather, say only the tundra

is sinking, the ice is moving
further away, she can't predict

what a dab will do: now
it looks like a candy-cane,

now the earth burned pink
to under-skin, enflamed.

When the earth is burnt, it doesn't wound,
why? The corpses of animals leave

blackened stains. She thumbs
off their remains. Blears

the passages between brush-strokes.
I returned to my vomit, that is

to say, I rewrote the last page.
She flips the canvas upside-down.

Revises a snowfield, drowns
the view-plane.

Wildfires lick the land
of little sticks into charcoal.

She extends herself
into plum-varnished sky.

The prettiness of the tundra
doesn't satisfy: she swabs at it

with wet wipes. Self-destruction
is the taiga lifestyle.

So, too, resurrection.
That burn-line above the lake:

SONG OF THE JEALOUS BIRD

In this perpetual
April light, how drab,
my garments. But not you,
my baby, my bunting, indigo,
or you the scarlet
tanager. I'm jealous,
birds. You undo
my buttons. Rest, you say,
but there's much
to protect, so I sing night
and day, no matter that it comes
out as sobbing. And your buzz
and chortle. Don't cross
over this line, bobolink,
white-crowned sparrow.
Birch trees, I drink your sap, I cast
a spell lest the telephone
ring, and you all asquabble.
Test me now. Why, you've
a glaucous gown, a veil
of ambition. Who shall
you wed, oh black-
backed woodpecker, oh violet-
green swallow? Succor of snowmelt
to hold you under. Silence
the jabber, whippoorwill,
big mouth talker. Here, and here,

I mark my trails, with these bright
acoustics and this my
cape of rare feathers, skins
of small, precious birds
I've murdered.

SINGS THE SELF IN ALL HER CHAINS

Squinting through black-framed glasses, she's gluing
her dead mother's frayed linen curtains to a canvas.
She's mixing the titanium white, the alizarin crimson.
She's regarding the jar of brushes, the bag of rags.
In the dense clump of trees out her window, there's one
tree she calls her self. The trunk dense with instinct
and claw-mark, she wants to paint that.

She's seventy, would rather not consider so much the self.
She wishes to paint what's larger, oneness, death. Frightened
to see the tree out there, separate from her body.
Wind passing through its branches. And light. Passing.
Meanwhile the body double in black, sensible shoes,
a blue ribbon holding her hair back, a gnarled hand
(is it hers, really?) reaches for a brush.

She paints in the others: outside her studio, in her kitchen
daughters, husband. Self as woman in labor, wife, mother.
Hidden she of a field where a dead lover's ashes are scattered,
the one who sang summer into her ear. Summer sings
now into all of her ears. Summer, the woods she wanders in,
summer, the death she paints not into but against. She adds black.
The tree steps forward, and she meets it. The art

of her self: every anatomical feature: trunk,
leaf, branch, bark, tree which goes not
gentle into that long winter night, which she loves,

also but secretly. The husband who jabbers nonsense in her ear,
riddles, puns, limericks, gossip, critique, is asleep upstairs.
Outside her window, the tree—it is silent. Inside, not so.
She paints her self in all her chains, to its green.

THE CLEARING

It would be spring. I'd be out walking.
I'd stumble across a field in a clearing.
A shock in the woods I thought I knew.
There'd be my mother wielding a hoe.

I'd stumble across her in the clearing.
Smoke from a stovepipe: her sister cooking.
There'd be my mother wielding a hoe.
She wouldn't be wearing a slip or stockings.

Smoke from the stovepipe: her sister cooking.
Nights they'd drink sting-nettle tea.
They'd be barefoot, no slips or stockings.
I'd call—but they wouldn't hear me.

Nights they'd drink sting-nettle tea.
As if it had always been this placid.
I'd call—but they wouldn't hear me.
The jokes they'd tell, dark and ironic.

As if it had always been this placid.
As if it had always been this place.
The jokes they'd tell, dark and ironic.
They wouldn't be raped—they'd be safe.

As if it had always been this place.
As if there'd been no reason to beg.
They wouldn't be raped—they'd be safe.
Under her dress, my mother's strong bare legs.

As if there had never been reason to beg.
Beside the woodstove, the little hatchet.
Under her dress, my mother's strong bare legs.
Where it was ripped, the careful stitches.

Beside the woodstove, the little hatchet.
Beside the door, a man's shoes.
Where it was ripped, the careful stitches.
While the kindling popped and the tea cooled.

Beside the door, a man's shoes.
Where have they gone, those men?
As the kindling popped and the tea cooled.
Song of a night-jar, song of a wren.

It would be spring. I'd be out walking.
A shock in the woods I thought I knew.
I'd stumble across a house in a clearing.
My mother stepping into the sun.

INSTRUCTIONS TO THE HUSBAND

Teach me what goes first: the pushki
or the devil's club, how August

dries the poison. What's the balm
for the welting nettle? Tell me how to marry

this chunk of earth, over which the wind
prevails, the seasons: mud

& crack-up. Instruct me
in the plant lore, the insect life, the medicines.

Carry me across the threshold
of lyme grass. Inspect my coat & pant legs

for evidence of transgression in
the overflow. Show me the seeds

that cling. When wool cape, when
gum boots. When snow shoes. When flip

flops. What are the native
plants here? How to identify

alien weeds. The toxic fungus, the edible
drupe. Where to find all-heal.

What does the soil want? Where to put
my mouth? When hot, when dry. Gentle or

not. Direct my gaze demurely down
to the scum of aphid, of spider mite.

Wasp nest. Shrew's den.
Tutor me in the husbandry

of cow moose, how to satisfy
the bear's need. Teach me how to live here.

Yes, my eyes are open.

THE EGG COUPLETS

Only one egg today when I trudged out to throw
slop to the hens, scatter ash on the path.

It's February, the sun's coming back and now
when he hears my voice, Olaf throws his head back

and crows. Big yellow man towers over his girls
like a coach, gives me the yellow eye.

The egg was green. I pocketed it, refilled
the water trough, scattered cracked corn. Tomorrow

I'll wake to the smell of a buttery concoction
the teens fry up, a protein storm of eggs and bacon.

But the egg was better in the pocket of my coat
that smells like a barn. Uncracked, shit-stained, still warm.

No, the egg was better in its bed of straw,
me kneeling, reaching, my fingers closing around.

Or best unseen, descending the fallopian tube
of the Araucana hen, announced by a string of bawls.

Now that I've traced it back, I realize
it was sweetest before it happened.

I walked to the coop on two strong legs
lugging a watering can and a bucket of feed.

The coop was there, the six chickens all accounted for.
Even the geriatric, Rhoda, who once in a while still

squeezes out a bullet-shaped double-yolker.
No owl devouring the hens as in my dream.

My knees bent, I scrunched myself into the opening
of the nesting shed and reached.

My arms and legs did what my mind said.
Birch trees scattered their tiny seeds.

The sun cleared the net of trees, a bleary yolk
in an egg-white froth of fog over the bay.

Walking back the dog waited for me,
the egg was warm in my pocket.

My house was there. And I was there,
and the egg for my family. Death was

nowhere foraging in the cottonwood trees.
Now I kneel in front of the stove

raking the ashes for a few live coals
to start the evening fire. I just walked

to the chicken coop and back.
That was all. I placed an egg in the tray

that marks a string of days laid out like that.
A life lived out, egg by egg. It was pretty good.

POISON BOUQUET

after handshakes, rice, waltzes, clinks
of glasses, there will be wormwood in mason jar vases

Artemisia tiessii—the stem *floccose, dental perfect, pappus, none*—dry,
indehiscent fruits—achenes—grown glabrous, devoid of hairs
or down, gown or crown, with age, like dowagers,
not brides—the wormwood the sisters picked
for the bridal bouquet pleased their scruffy hearts.

For the bride to wear wormwood
in her hair & for the wild arrangements: *Achillea,*
yarrow wound in tight boutonnieres
dropping pollen and duff on banquet tables, nodding
their heads like virgin cousins sharing secrets through the long speeches.

Green skullcaps opening to yellow umbels: for those they ranged
through town wielding paring knives,
scissors flashing, harvesting fleabane, sheaves
of sedge, filling their five-gallon pails.

They discarded the delicate, no gladioli, peonies,
no futzing with garden blooms. There would be wild things.
Wormwood would poison
the bouquet with need, leave scratchy seeds
on the marriage bed. On the wedding night,
and nights to come (if the sisters had their way)
those gods would hunger down and keep
the bride dreaming and awake.

2. CORDELIA, DISOBEDIENT, SINGS HER SONGS

. . . for the human kingdom, beneath the floor of the comparatively neat little dwelling that we call our consciousness, goes down into unsuspected Aladdin caves; there not only jewels but dangerous jinn abide: the inconvenient or resisted psychological powers that we have not thought or dared to integrate into our lives. And . . . some chance word, the smell of a landscape, the taste of a cup of tea, or the glance of an eye may touch a magic spring, and then dangerous messengers begin to appear in the brain. These are dangerous because they threaten the fabric of the security into which we have built ourselves and our family. But they are fiendishly fascinating too, for they carry keys that open the whole realm of the desired and feared adventure of the discovery of the self.

—Joseph Campbell, from *The Hero With a Thousand Faces*

How to separate out the chains from the bonds, the harms from the value, the truth from the lies.

—Tillie Olsen, from *Silences*

I.

Sometimes there's Cordelia asleep,
comma-shaped in the garden beneath
the birdbath, simple as an egg laid & left

before an eye opens before stretch
& thought & what? & huh? & time?
before *oh shit* there's her ear,

comma-shaped & blank & the flycatcher
with its randy song & black mask
calling her back & no sentence, no syntax,

no line, no kiss, only this: the stone-on-stone
scritch of a slate pencil, her at eight, writing
on a rock at the creek beside her jar of pollywogs,

that *saw-saw* wakes her, announces
its genus, its species, its vermillion, olive-
sided, scissor-tailed, Acadian, ash-throated,

yellow-bellied, willow, whatever—
she's deaf to all but its scrape, a dull
blade on salt-encrusted beach-cast Cordelia's

inner ear, now she's hauling herself up &
back inside—oh bliss, this—hatched, thus—
out of nothing—empty of need

to sit at her loom or to build a fire.

II.

Linnaeus, you disappoint, the father said. Consider
the portrait of young Carl on a botanical expedition
to Lapland in 1731, wearing a traditional Lapp costume,
beating a shaman's drum. What a fake! Linnaeus inspecting
sex parts, counting pistils, stamens, examining sheaths.
He should have been a priest. Instead he called the sexless
Cryptograma, "plants of hidden marriage," the algae, the lichens,
the fungi, the moss. The mossy wife he disappointed.
Linnaeus come back to bed! she pleaded. While he labored
over his floral clock, reckoned time by the closing
of petals. Claiming sepals as bridal beds, dividing and naming
as he went, he headed north without looking back. Waving nomenclature
                like an ax. The gods put Linnaeus on her track.
                Lying in the grass, Cordelia dreamed him.

III.

How is it the common briar rose came not to be known
as *Rosa sylvestris alba cum rubore, folio glabro,*
but dubbed by close inspection of the sex,
Rosa canina? Linnaeus botanicus, you beguile
the world with your pairings.
How will you tell when the lusty
leaves disappear, which is glabrous, which is fair?
Do you count black fair? Winter will
confound you, nature's butcher's block
unman the names and ranks. *Homo diurnis,*
man of the day, the further north you go,
the longer the names.

IV.

Now she remembers buttons she has to push or sew on.
Now she remembers the awkward way his hand landed, trying to act
accidental, like a bird that mistook her boot-tip for its branch.
Now she remembers how to adjust the position of
a bird alive in the hand. Now she remembers how you can run after
the bitter end of a line and try and catch it before it sails off the dock.
Now she remembers the caught look on a man's face.
Now she remembers the flour, the sugar, the cinnamon,
the water. Now the shape of a schooner,
deck-loaded, Pacific gushing through its scuppers.
Now the happiness of order, a taxonomical
key to flora, all the names of flowers' parts.

                    Now she remembers a fat and parenthetical moment
                    climbing onto the schooner, not looking back.

V.

lord unmake me—erase me—recreate me invisible—yes—
mouse brown—tide come back—be silt—dust on
the piano lid—make me dander make me owl shit—give me back—my body
unwrapped from this sweater—make me beluga-gray-skinned in
the gray-skinned inlet—let me be microscopic—see how
someone saw that wave & called it me—(yes like that)—
how someone named me boneless named me thin-skinned
lackluster—hid me under a rock & you (interpreter of taxonomy)—
turned the rock—even wetting your hands first—as if you—(!)—
knew the possibility of—(but still the doing of—) studied me—
(took notes in fact) put that rock (you thought)—exactly—
as you found it—but my lord—I was not—undisturbed—& this is not—
                    —this made/unmade animal you see—
                    is not the same—won't ever be—

VI.

Then she remembers *Systema Naturae*, how
in classifying—lens to the sex—thus in the name—
is found the order—the god's intention—for her,
for everything (!)—so: she is cleaning

the house, she is mopping the floor, she is sewing
the button onto the shirt, Cordelia is cooking something up—blood
pudding—she is getting ready—but it isn't working.
Cordelia thinking, *Did I forget father's day again?*

Cordelia back to the confessional. Back to the garden, the books.
Cordelia on her back, on the side, on top, upside-down &
under. But still the territory remains unmarked, untaken.

> *Bless me father for I have lied. There was no loom. I kept*
> *my ear pressed to the door the whole time, I was listening, I was*
> *waiting for a hand on my wrist, I was biting my lower lip till it bled.*

VII.

TO DO:

1—sew button back on his pants
2—mow lawn, trim edge
3—sonnet/argument/anti-thesis—what is a "subtle whore"??
4—pretend thesis:
4—Othello—jealousy, murder = stupid ass
5—check mail box
5—dust loom
5—let down cuffs
6—check cistern
7—slap Desdemona
8—answer question: is love an "ever-fixed sign"?
9—answer question: if you cry will I?
10—get "hot, hot, and moist", then get sequestered
11—come lay with me and be my _____
12—(tamed shrew)
13—thaw leg of lamb
13—forget to _____ distracted by _____
14—answer question: which rack of goodness would by ill taste best, last long?

VIII.

Soul, she prays, make a path through legs of lamb.
Cordelia as landing craft, pushes a wake
before her as she plows past
the mending. A few hopeful porpoises ricochet
off her bow wave, tossed aside. She runs
over various species of resting marine life.
Cordelia, over-loaded, not surge-protected, is herself
a surge. In overdrive, she drags her skirts
in the hours, wonders at birds making paths

through leaves. All she sees in the trees
are color patches stitched with black, to part
a swath before her would take
a clear-cut, a D-9 Cat. Soul make her go
gentle into that private, into that green
god, pure, skirting branches, sure

as shit as birds are sure. Dodging
obstacles like *lust*, like *male attention*,
like *affirmation*, like *settledness*
like *shopping list*, like *twelfth step*, her entire
view taken up with green in shadow
in glare—go girl, disappear
into that leaf-thrash vegetal
mosh-pit, tangled, but with openings,
                              openings, everywhere:

IX.

—in which Cordelia bumps up against the laws

Law #1: The house should be homey, with antique furniture & herbs, vines, orchids, books, fires, concrete counters (i.e. French country), two cats in yard, henhouse, signs of mother.

Law #2: The house should be Polynesian, simple basketry, bare wood, Japanese screens.

Law #3: The house should be Zen, breezy with feng shui. Shovel the clutter into a cardboard box. Chop back the vines. One orchid on a low table. Ditch the cats. Open window to rain and chi. Remove extra cutlery.

Law #4: The house should be messy, dirty dishes stacked up, dust on the piano lid. Obvious signs of poverty, woman too busy at her loom to stay clean (butts, cuttings, threads).

Law #5: The house should be Alaskan, nailed-up snow-shoes, woodstove, geraniums in murky windows, lots of out-of-print hard-covers on shelves.

Law #6: The house should be artistic. Stash realism in basement. Make it funky, abstract paintings, Mexican tin, miniature teapot collection.

Law #7: The house should be smaller. The windows don't seal. The cats have ripped the weather-stripping. Invest in solar. Start over.

Law #8: The house should look like a Navajo hogan.

Law #9: There is too much too much too much stuff in house. It should weigh about 8 oz.

Law #10: Bare floors, sheer curtains blowing in breeze, mattress on floor (white organic cotton bedding), just a few poetry books.

Law #11: Church-like, incense, candles stuck in wine bottles, dripping wax, blue glass, plenty icons, prayer mats.

Law #12: Everything entirely of natural materials. Yogurt in jar under heat-lamp under sweater. Sills decorated with beach stones & feathers. Loose-leaf tea.

> Homeless, she considers her options. How shall she be?
>
> Of leather, of henhouse, of chokecherry tree?

X.

Since you came an eye is in my mind,
and what instructs me to go into the garden
compels but I'm half-blind, finding,
with half an eye, chickweed tangled in black
clover, pulling the stem but never the root,
brushing my hands, leaving it half-done, for where
I once saw dandelion apart from lily,
jewelweed from Jacob's ladder, now the heart
recognizes no art in splitting weed from herb,
heal-all from nettle, science from beauty, defies
the infernal naming, cheats on Linnaeus who burns
the weeds black with his propane cannon,

half the eye lost in yes, love, half
hiding in the shadows.

XI.

Given green perfume. Given talks about sex.
Given a cunt in which to tuck the unsaid.
Given a face which will not hide
but can put a meditative look on the face
of a secret & a body that tells & tells.
Given an oboe into which, for a time,
a secret can be blown. Given a bottle
into which, for a time, a secret can be cried.

Given a cigarette, a secret can be burned.
Given a cervix, a secret attaches, watches the scenery
from its stalk. Given language, a secret can dissemble.
Given form. Given simile. Given stanza.
Given lines. A secret can lie
beneath leaf-death and molder.
Given a third person whose voice may
or may not be drowned by the din
of territorial birds.

Or the wind and leaves secreting the secret away.

XII.

I concede. I enter you naked, forest. Change me. I duck beneath
your branch & my skin darkens like water & your breath cools
the skin of my forearms & ankles like water. I always thought

someone else passed here & left this chill but it was you –
I enter, I'm willing, change me. Here's my trowel. I'll dig randomly
for a tuberose, for a moccasin flower, for club moss,

for poison. For the dark one, green & not so tender, I enter you,
change me, make me animal, derange me.
The deer here are small, their paths narrow, but I'll crawl, I'll do

anything you ask. On my hands & knees it's more like water, this green,
so littoral. Has science changed me? Has God? Our lady of weeds.
I'm through with her now, change me. I enter you virginal.

Without clue or key. Here, only one kind
of intelligence matters, one kind
of beauty. Show me: where the light is, where, the water.

XIII.

The bog-pond by which she sat,
in the muskeg, on a matt of moss & flytrap soaking
in tannic, wasn't it the lover's face
into which she sank? Moving a strand
of hair from her face, the skin ruddy,
not soft as a leaf, the body lean, not gravid as a spring
deer, fed on skunk cabbage
clothed in crowberry, all those low-
growing plants, her legs tucked under, leaning
on her hand, looking, not recognizing
who, calling, a bird . . . dipping
her fingers in, watching
her face shatter
& reform . . .
No, adamant, it's a pond,
no stranger, it's nature actual, unnamed,
unmanned, no metaphor, no lure,
a pond drinking in desire
as only water can, swallowing
all she gives, refracting, offering it,
even in the dark, back from its face,
from its depth, more than she can stand,
more than anyone can stand . . .

XIV.

The boreal forest, bug-infested, asked to be seen, clad itself
in tight jeans, suggested the primitive nomenclature.

The forest voluptuous without shame showed itself
to Linnaeus, how could he refrain? *See me, vascular.*

See my ligules entire, glumes appressed. Touch to discern
 whether glabrous or scabrous my lemmas, how prominently nerved.

(The wife never had a chance). See the coarse grass.
 The awn long, soft, the awn thick, stiff.

Linnaeus not doomed to near-sightedness:
the plant press, the hand lens. As he looked

he touched. As he touched he named. As he named everything
changed. Like a wood frog burrowed underneath

the autumn duff, he lost his mind's frame. Say it plain:
Linnaeus fell ass over fringe cup, he fell all the way.

XV.

In wilderness, mirrors wait. Sunk in ponds,
half-truths lie in state. Arms to the elbows
reach into the sponge of bogs, retrieve
the bones of lovers, pickled
in the acid stink. In muskeg footprints
linger. Selves wander, heavy with freight.
Keying wildflowers. Trampling plants.
Arctic this. Fringed that. Recording notes

in yellow books: false hellebore buds late.
Chocolate lily smells like diapers, makes
bitter rice. Devil's club root will purify.
Where does beauty reside? In the eye that regards
reindeer lichen? That eye aches. Because
beauty won't sustain. It will equal 0 not X.
It will be eternal thirst.

XVI.

& then I came into a gravelly place, an opening
in the head-high grass & I lay down. My ears throbbed
from the pressure of the silence all around. Here no metaphor
no metaphysical conceit. Plants moved up & around in wind.
A red squirrel chirred, scaring off a great gray owl. In my ears,
a humming sound: spruce tips moving over me a thousand times.
I was through with imaginings. The place was all that mattered.
I died then. My head got heavy & my skin got tight. Wind filled
the remnant spaces with leaves' whisperings, water's murmurings,
they'd never stop. I stopped. But my other self, the third person,
she got up. There was a smell like over-turned peat. She forgot
all the names. She was the tree & she was splayed,
like the fern. Pond and bog flame. Observed, observer, leaf
& lover. She was witness. She was water.

3. I PREFER WINTER

I prefer winter. The internal, the mental, the dream, the book, the obscure, the difficult, the private, the brief, the brilliant, the episode, the event, the quick kiss in frost air . . . The body wears protective garb. Only the face is exposed, eyes alert, mouth pursed, skin dry and thin, parchment frail. You might glimpse a person's soul.

—Ann Lauterbach, from "The Night Sky VI"

AND GOD OPENED A WINDOW

And there's a north wind in it.
And a few houses with lights on
    sprinkled over the day that we'll eat.
And the view plane lightening and there's a little
    death in it, settling behind the knees of animals.
And an orange stain bleeds out of a ridgeline
    but everywhere else it only gets bluer.
And the morning plane slices into it
    as it banks toward Anchorage.
And the crowns of trees are all connected in it.
And crows don't care, they just burst right through it.
In the killing cold a search plane looking down on it
    would see small fires moving across the landscape.
And bigger fires, human beings constructing
    themselves every morning from sticks and paper.
We forget that through infrared glasses we all look equal.
Forget we could walk into that scene,
    meet death halfway to where we're going and not
    sit in our houses waiting.
Because when God opened a window something had to be done.
Walking into the landscape, the faithful are departing.
This is the far-off country I'm writing to you from.

YOU DARKNESS

after Rilke

October darkness (can't)
take me in, tap at my window, lure
me to your half-bitten frost-light
(rose fringe) over new snow, over
mountain snout, sleep, gentle, open
your mouth, you my lord of leaf fall
(of whitening), take this,
(unforgiven) down the trail through
meadows, down the eroded gully
(my thoughts) and as I watch
(softest parts flushing)
most horizon, cold to the edge—
ridgeline—glacial tongue,
take my mind, darkness
(that I cannot love) & I'll step into
the alders, under the goshawk's killing
tree (above me, looking through & past
—flayed beneath—picked clean) be not
so pretty, so pink, erasure
who unfolds, holds this (madness)
pressed in the swale, creek bed
(jealous lover) take me cold and hard.
Still this (something) comes (not) asking
for my logical, into this (my private),
demon lover you are below the horizon,
blue as a black eye.

DAZZLED ON THE TUNDRA

look—there's a dazzle on the tundra—something unexpected—unexplained—
with light behind it—something that almost (should have) happened—(sex in a
rainstorm)—(an unexpected landform)—(the ice pack, winking)

—scrutinize it—the vein in bedrock—the crack in a formation—an accident of
seeing—(track of wing in snow)—stacked stones—(someone, something, was)—
shaped by ice exposed to drumming—that something that makes the world seem
strange—makes an animal blink—(and if it blinks this will)—not be—not last—

(not so fast, naturalist)—no—wait like a figure on the sea ice—(be that still)—
hunter—perceive what is not yet given—until—(circle back)—he waits by the
breathing hole—whistling through his teeth—the way he ties a knot without
seeing—approach the animal—without looking—in its face—

(do you see—that dazzle—now)—?

DISPATCH

Today I'm standing on top of that mountain.
The one you see from your kitchen window.
Every morning when you drink your tea.
Every morning when you brush your teeth.
Today the wind is brushing the twigs.
The twigs and leaves from my hair.
I'm standing knee-deep.
Knee-deep in snow, I'm over my head.
Clouds above me and below.
Everyonceinawhile a surprised-looking bird.
A bird hurtling west toward the Barren Islands.

The storm's south wall just careened past.
Dragging a jib, a hatch cover, a scuttle.
There goes a container ship
spilling its contents: cargo
of sneaker and fortune tellers.
I'm dodging debris.
I'm falling down the mountain.
I'm crawling back up.
Repeatedly.
I'm singing.
Singing in spite
of the noise all around.
The noise in my head, the noise of flinging.
And the noise of my breathing.
The storm tears the lyrics out of my head.
Through the hole in my head the storm is passing.
Sheets of white slinging buckets of blue.

There's another mountain higher than this one.
You can see it through a hole in the blue.

That's where I'm going, bucking the headwind.
I'm not where you think I am.
I'm not where I said I'd be.
I'm there, on the mountain, in a new
kind of pain.

IT BEGINS IN ICE

I don't know what we expect to find: something blue
& pretty, not how the world begins in ice, not how it's still
being created. Here past & future exactly the same.

How we float in between slickensides, our fingers poking
out of fingerless gloves. We belong to the older world,
clad & lush. This creation of our country, chaotic, wild,

doesn't recognize us. We weren't born yet. The ice pulls back
unlike a tide, exposing nothing alive, just natal parts:
Rock flour, newborn scree, a template for the first lichen.

The glacier's intelligence is unfathomable to us.
Who, hiking up the moraine to where the ground's barren
could feel at home pitching a tent in a field of debris?

Even the alder thickets don't invite us to build a fire,
squat with a mug of smoky tea, listening to the one
sparrow claim his undisputed terrain over & over.

In the morning, we pack to go & we're relieved, hearing
sudden cracks as a face gives way, unloading another wall
of Jesus ice into the innocent milk of the fjord.

There are places on earth that aren't our home, scenery
about which, cameras cocked, we can't say, "When you look
at this, you can see forever," and not be afraid.

Here past and future always backing away, leave us
marooned. If we put our ear to the ground,
we won't be reassured. We don't belong here. We never did.

THIS IS THE FAR-OFF COUNTRY
I'M WRITING TO YOU FROM

Here God's a mean man. He takes us every night in his spade-shaped teeth
& holds on. His jaw often aches. He gets frequent migraines.

Here the forest is greedy. Roots burrow under lawns & suck rain. On bare spots
fungi open their shameless faces.

Here the forest sleeps & wakes like an animal & doesn't believe
in saving daylight. Here animals are furnaces dragging across the landscape, chewing.

Here we wake in the dark & don't know the time.

I'm here to tell you that we exist. We wear wool scarves & pin up our hair.
We wear big earthy sweaters & thick socks & overcoats & boots lined with fur

& we wear all of that inside. We believe in the layered look.
It's one of the commandments.

God looks right at us here, whereas he sees you through a mist.
There's nothing between God & us, the blue's so thin, so clear.
We brush shoulders with him every day. He hunts where we do.
He has incredibly big ears.

He sits beside us on bleachers & cheers for children racing in a pool.
Naked children jump in the pool at night. God doesn't care about nudity here
& children don't care about death.

Sometimes he disguises himself as a girl who keeps lifting her dress
to show everyone her Cinderella underpants.

Sometimes with cold hands & red cheeks & a dreamy expression
on his childish face, he wanders around on the tundra.
Forgetting why he's here, the scenery's so vast & distracting.

It's very white here, & he likes that. People & animals have a lot of sex up here
& God's in on it.

In September we go into the dark like orphans being led onto jumbo jets
to be taken to far-off countries not knowing why
& it happens again & again.
We're used to it. We buckle our seat belts without being told.

You can be a cowboy here. At forty-below, you can be a lineman
 & work with hot, juicy wires. You can die any number of ways,
by water, by ice, by fire.

This is the big one. You only get a little cream skimmed off, a whiff
when the wind blows just the right way.

Some say the world will end in ice. In the far-off country I'm writing to you from,
it's beginning in ice,
it's beginning right now,
& it's coming your way.

THE ICE OF NORTON SOUND, REFUSING

for Kristine

Like any fixation, any obsessive
collecting, it's steeped in a specialized

language. She tries to catch each
word on her tongue, taste each separate

fragment. She closes her eyes like one pretending
to know how to describe the aftertastes

of wines: abrasive—the frazil,
slithery—the grease, the hiccup

of shuga, this process she repeats, learning
the lingo, then studying the guides,

identifying the mammals, the plants.
But now there are no plants, just

shadows, no colors, just hues
of transparency, grays that haven't

been identified. So she keeps a life list
of phenomena: water sky, ice blink,

kapsik, pressure ridge, avalanche
of pack ice barreling down

the Bering Strait to make of the sea
an anxious self. So she embarks

uninformed, terrified, without
a lexicon or pencil, strapping on

snow shoes, heading straight to where
a lead splits the frozen sea in two,

a place where knowing
ends, where language founders,

where wind carries off all her word
endings. Remember that edge,

ships plunging off explorers' maps,
& someone's marked the margin: *Here there be . . . ?*

But the crucial part's worn away—?
Remember? That's where she begins.

No received notion of ice or self, no ecology
ties the jammed maze together.

She finds no edge, just the fractured remains
of ice that once held a shape, her shape, ice

of endless kinds, refusing to be named.

GHAZAL OF THE MADMAN'S CHILD

My father used the wind
to gauge our fate:
Zephyr, Boreus, Notus, Eurus. Is my fate

a gale-snapped branch?
On my tongue, I test the hypothesis that
place is fate:

Linden tree. Snow bell.
Devil's grass. Is fate

permission to name everything? Cracked
taxonomist, he
traced his fate

back to distinct stars,
the sky's hand-made lace. If fate

is appetite, explain my dislike
for tinned eel, pickled herring,
plaice. Is fate

accusatory? My father jabbed his finger
at me. Life is perpetual
displacement. His fate

the hitch-hiked tongue, its
broken phonic: *kokle, puce, laima, roka.*

My father's
suitcase is not my fate.

She loved his tongue-tied
Americanisms. In case of a case, he said.
As in, in case of a suitcase, my fate

can be found rolled up in a wad of dollar bills, stuck
in the left pocket
of my woolen jacket.
In lace, is fate

the holes? I mistook the time
it would take to relearn his language.
In Latvian, how to say: his path you couldn't
retrace. Is fate

forgetting? Is it a stone rolled
on the tongue?
Or off? A word no force of nature can
erase? Is fate

shoeless? Does it carry a passport?
It's a sin-eater. It's a brief case.
It's the hunger of empty manila folders.
Also praise. Yes.
Praise is fate.

Divine it how you like: tea leaves,
tarot cards, a shoelace. Fate

is unforeseeable, like wind. Cordelia,
your father tried to see that wind.
Forgive him.

4. TO A WORLD WITHOUT NAME, AMEN

Imagine . . . an eye which does not respond to the name of everything . . . Imagine a world alive with incomprehensible objects and shimmering with an endless variety of movement and innumerable gradations of color. Imagine a world before "the beginning was the word."

—Stan Brakhage, *Metaphors on Vision*

MANY WAYS TO SAY IT

They come to the lake and it's brimming its bank.

The sun's at the edge of a cloudbank.

The cloudbank slowly cruising west.

A wren chattering in the alder.

Midges, flies, dragonflies zinging over the lake.

In this light, legs are bluish.

He begins as the cloudbank bypasses.

Grasses swaying in an imperceptible breeze.

They are lying in the grasses.

With another across the lake, the wren arguing.

A vortex of midges rises from the grass.

The cloudbank draws south, pulling back the shadows from their feet.

Chalk marks rubbed into blue: a few cirrus clouds.

What are you writing about, he asks.

(Bears trampled the saltbush).

The lush grass.

Fireweed cotton blowing all around.

Caught in the web strung between two blades of grass.

Birds chipping, chipping away at the silence.

The south wind pushing the lake water north.

A stem curled around the inner thigh.

High clouds drawing a veil across the sun.

He turns. *Take off your blouse.*

Scalloped—all through the cloudbank.

Legs apart, the sun between them.

The coupled dragonflies somersaulting through the clouds of midges

are also a way of saying.

Then they swim.

BACKLIT/INLET

Up from the light

Of the body (the bay):

Aluminum sheet creased

Where fishing boats

Slit the bore tide.

Clouds spiked by

Rusty nails of dead spruce

Tack north, rinse oxides

Off the slopes.

What Christ

Died for all this? That creeping

Cloud-strip, the sea's

Dull sheen. Dark lips

Of isthmus. Lack

(of wind). And someone,

Sporadically, hammering

A roof on.

ALIZARIN

Begin behind the coop between the beehive
& the fence where the ground is spackled
yellow-green-brown, where washed out leaflets
topple, umbrellas sprung, sun-bleached underfoot,
under your rubber boots: the field: light tipped, ferns
gone bad, nettles limp: stripped

to brown the whole meadow soft
(breeze from north) says
yes to the hidden place: there: where the light
falls between reddish veins
on the undersides of leaves, kneel
in mud not frozen (not indirect)
(to ask) but the earth
can't never (not) say (*lie with me*
in poison, in mustard) & your face
(one leaf) falling to the cheek
on the spotted trail
in sickness
answers yes:

        & now float

(spent leaf)   upside-down   on the tea-stains
of the stagnant
pond

& walking back you're leaf-jangling
just a scrap of human left

enough for (*yes*) (listen): as water
louder downhill under breathes in sleep
a sulfury smell of in betweens
& light flicks off the leafless
clumps of devil's club
in a blaze
of alizarin, now say it,
(say you will)
i will

MY MOUNTAIN

—after Stan Brakhage

of leaves twisting into wings of weather posturing the leaves going nowhere the snow blowing leaves sideways devolving the sky slanting the stones wind prying sky flying the slope reddening yellowing browning lapsing clouds erasing my mountain clattering branches rattling scree snow lengthening ground hardening stones falling the mountain loosening the stones its grip the snow its white the wind ripping the leaf its hold the cold tightening bluing my mountain until my mountain sinking into the muskeg, disappears:

(where my mountain when & if & then my mountain undressing my mountain unclouding shushing my mountain baring solidifying evaporating my mountain elaborating my mountain fabricating sheering my mountain yielding stiffening my mountain dangerous taking dissolving my alpine tiny my alpine specific lichening with small leaves gesticulating my mountain bravado brave)

deflowering seeping asleep the snow running the slopes leaching the white blackening the buds reddening the wind pinching fingering battering the slopes green swollen with _____

tattooing my mountain wet my mountain undone exposed pierced the shadows tucking under beside

the mountain low, above & below, again, now & then, always my mountain
never
my mountain

WHAT ENDURES

All day buds open in late spring light.
On the pond, a gleam, a mote,
a wrinkle. Where we lie
sleeping, in dry grass, snowshoe
hares leap by on white feet,
with white ears.

Words (hard or soft) don't last.
Even when flakes
drift past us so thick
they seem to stand still
and we are falling—
it's all gone by mid-morning.

This is not a love poem
to what lasts. Not to the pulse
under the cup in the breastbone,
not grace, but the endless offering of a place
to lie down—a nap by the squirrel
midden, sex by the unnamed
stream, where small rustlings
happen and you forget
your sunglasses.

MOTHER WATER

The Erie of my youth was powder blue
and young, or old and rabbit gray, or wild, or ice-locked
like a paternal jaw. Its lake effect: white
scream of blizzard, then silence. Fridays, we ate
its whitefish fried, its herring brined,
in the old country way. It was our Baltic.

Hot summer afternoons my mother
took us to the lake to play, the sky yellow,
thunder impending, waves overhead.
At Sunset Bay some days a dried up carp
or sucker offered up
an eyeless socket to our sticks.

In bikinis we ducked rogue
waves, worried lampreys would
latch to our legs. Weathered
glass collecting, we toed dead pumpkinseeds,
knowing well the lake's myth: how once, betrayed
it died. Then was resurrected.
Every three years, it's new again.
Except that a lifeless eye every summer
forms in the lake and drifts, a lost planet.

What pretty poem or platitude,
what prayer is sufficient to a lake
so shallow you can walk a quarter mile

and never get your shoulders wet?
It was no sea, no Adriatic, no Pacific.
Not pristine or blessed, it was mother-water

nonetheless, second-rate, working class, badly used,
a flat horizon to a Canada I couldn't see
on the clearest days. In it I was baptized.
My skin exudes its carp perfume.

NO AUDIENCE

I'd like to be the only one awake
this afternoon on the boat, weathered in
by this Bering Sea storm. The wind

gusting to 45, the others
in their bunks, snoring. I'd be chewing
through an entire pack of gum, reading

poems, trying to write
one out of nothing
but the kettle's hiss, the GPS,

the lurch of the boat in a squall.
I'd like to be the one
on anchor watch, glassing

the impassable seas outside
the cove for spouts and
dorsal fins, spotting

the rain-soaked coat of the bruin
pawing and nosing the wrack
for whale fat, I'd be marking it down

in a notebook: 1 bruin.
I'd be inserting it
in my poem—right here: [brown bear]

I'd like to be drinking tea,
cup after cup, getting up every 15 minutes
to pee or to do 30 sit-ups. And no one

watching. To pick up
a pencil, take down a sighting
of 2 Steller sea lions at 1500, to transcribe

the lat and long in the log.
To scan the seas for a finned or winged
insight. When the boat swings

into the wave's trough, I'd like to be
the one to see that williwaw
smack down on the bay, and the bay

throw the williwaw right back up
into the sky's face, I'd like to be
the one who'd try

to get that into a poem,
and there'd be no one to read it.
I'd like to be here, right now,

with something to tell,
and no one to hear it.

THE LOVER

Always the firm pressure
Of scraggy, lichened boulders,
Always, the stubble and coarseness of moss.
Always the conversation
Of water or bird, its complaint,
Its news, its story-telling.
Always the damp, flexing limbs,
Heady smells nose-deep in ground cover.
Always the body, willing, the welcome.
Always its gifts, corpses of seabirds,
Sometimes only the gray wings.

IF ONLY THE MIND

for pleasure solely skimming

the way updraft—a phenomenon

of physics lifts these gulls—in and out of fog

a few quick

up-thrusts, then *forget it*—

if the mind changed

course suddenly—   if the flapping

stopped—

rocket-fall   (level with cliff top)

—past the bunkers—

leaf litter in drifts—

a few feathers ruffling—

out of nothing: circling

the air column

(not a burden, the canted

wingspan)

& the mind:

far above the glaucous ceiling
by the orange-and-white day-marker.

MESSENGER

Like a mouth wanting to speak

to you, but there's a window between us.

Always an intermediary, no,

a messenger. Please take this message, bird.

This communiqué. To the mountain razored out of night.

To that line of peaks.

Storms approach but send

no signal, so sudden, a dab

of night in a puddle of water. Do you know

what I mean? No. For you, bird, the rules

do not apply.

My tongue sticks

to the window glass. Meanwhile the day

is spreading, the day is running

out on me. Earth, be

my point zero.

Mountain strip down for me.

Take this

message, bird. Don't

be like his truck barreling up the road,

so urgent, he's splashing his coffee. Hers, the red truck

galloping down the opposite way.

Yearnings criss-crossed.

Marks missed. Meanings lost

in a mess of alders.

See, my bird, you

over-shot. Go back! Let me be perfectly clear,

perfectly plain. Dot. Dot. Dash. Up and under

the arc of a branch. Take this message, bird.

Be quick. Deliver it to my lover.

BIOGRAPHICAL NOTE

Eva Saulitis, an essayist, poet, and marine biologist, has studied the killer whales of Prince William Sound, Alaska for twenty-five years. Her first book, *Leaving Resurrection: Chronicles of a Whale Scientist* (Boreal Books/Red Hen Press, 2008), was a finalist for the Tupelo Press Non-Fiction Prize and the ForeWord Book Award. Her second non-fiction book, *Into Great Silence*, is forthcoming from Beacon Press. A recipient of writing fellowships from the Rasmuson Foundation and the Alaska State Council on the Arts, she is an associate professor in the University of Alaska Low-Residency MFA program.